Covered Animal Dishes

Everett Grist

COLLECTOR BOOKS

A Division of Schroeder Publishing Co., Inc.

The current values in this book should be used only as a guide. They are not intended to set prices, which vary from one section of the country to another. Auction prices as well as dealer prices vary greatly and are affected by condition as well as demand. Neither the Author nor the Publisher assumes responsibility for any losses that might be incurred as a result of consulting this guide.

Searching For A Publisher?

We are always looking for knowledgeable people considered to be experts within their fields. If you feel that there is a real need for a book on your collectible subject and have a large comprehensive collection, contact us.

Additional copies of this book may be ordered from:

Collector Books
P.O. Box 3009
Paducah, KY 42002-3009

@$14.95. Add $2.00 for postage & handling.

Copyright: Everett Grist, 1988
Values Updated 1993

1 2 3 4 5 6 7 8 9 0

Printed by IMAGE GRAPHICS, INC., Paducah, Kentucky

Appreciation

I want to thank Stan and June Sohl for their help. Also the chicken lady (Mina Colvin), Bob Costa, my good friend Jim from Kansas and a special thanks to the brothers-in-law. Without their participation on that cold and cloudy October day, none of this would have been possible.

My First Encounter

On a cool fall morning in October about five years ago, Goldie and I attended a sale at the Five Mile House. I understand that the Five Mile House got its name because it is five miles south of Charleston and was once the first stage coach stop after leaving Charleston. I believe it was at one time a museum, but as far as I know, it was never open after I moved here. The ad describing the sale was not very interesting. Very little was mentioned that we might be interested in so we were late in arriving. As we walked up, the auctioneer called out "Hello Everett and Goldie." I thought this was quite unusual to greet us in the middle of a call. Then I realized he was asking for help.

"Look at the brothers-in-law," I said to Goldie. It was a few days later that she asked how I knew that group of men were brothers-in-law. Then I explained that they weren't really. It is a term used by the old auctioneers, especially in the South, to describe two or more people who have agreed not to bid against each other. There is nothing illegal about it, but I consider it unethical. The auctioneer hoped that I would jump in and help break it up.

I did just that, and it soon developed into another game – one even more senseless. I don't know what you call it, but the idea is for one bidder to run the other bidder up as high as possible above the value of the item being sold and then drop it on him without getting caught. Anyway, it was me pitted against the brothers-in-law and they were taking me one at a time. Needless to say, I was losing but every once in a while I would drop it on one of them. That would send him to the truck.

After the sale, the auctioneer walked up, shook my hand and thanked me for attending the sale. He told me I was top buyer and all the other little things that might make a man feel good after "squandering his riches."

While this was going on, Goldie was settling up with the cashier. "Well," I asked, "how much?" "$2,200.00," she said, good natured as usual. "What are we going to do with $2,200.00 worth of covered animal dishes?" "Oh, don't worry sweetheart," I said, "we're going to sell'em and make a whole lot of money."

Then I began to realize I didn't know what they were worth or how to price them. There were some rare ones I was sure – or at least several that I had not seen before.

So I started hunting for information, looking for books and asking my dealer friends a million questions.

A short time later we did a show in Kansas City. We were set up across the aisle from Stan Sohl. I knew Stan to be a dealer in covered animal dishes. This was my chance to get some real good firsthand information. I must have been a real pest as I was asking questions every spare moment during the 4-day show. I even recorded most of our conversations for future reference. He was very helpful and nice and to show my appreciation I bought several dishes that I did not have (somewhere around $1,000.00 worth) accepting his small discount without question.

My next major purchase was from my good friend Jim from Kansas. Having heard that I was buying covered animal dishes, he was waiting for me at the next show – $1,200.00 worth – retail he claimed. I thought he was a little high, but there were some nice pieces and I really wanted them. I also had some marbles that he really wanted. After four days of haggling, we traded marbles for the entire lot of covered animal dishes. We made a "perfect deal." A "perfect deal" is when a trade is made between two old pros like Jim and me and both of us walk away smiling and thinking "Well I really got the best of the old boy that time."

Now it was time to start displaying and selling my collection. Pricing was not an easy job because what I had paid didn't have much to do with the actual value of the dishes in most cases. I gathered all the information I could find and priced anyway. I showed them in about five shows with little results. I met Dr. Ferson, author of *Yeterday's Milk Glass Today*, in Pennsylvania and saw his collection. And he sold me an out-of-print copy of Millard's book on opaque glass. His comments was "A very impressive display but unrealistic prices."

After a few more shows, Goldie said to me "Have you noticed how religious the people are here?" "How's that, Sweetheart?" I asked. "Every time someone looks at one of your covered animal dishes and sees the price, they say "Oh my God!" she answered.

I got the message. I carefully packed my animal dishes and carried them to the storage shed and placed them beside all the other "bargains" we had bought in the last few years. That's where they remained until it was time to sort them to take to Paducah for photographing.

A wise old dealer once said, "You cannot pay too much for a good antique – but you can buy it too soon." Well, it seems I may have bought them a mite too soon.

This didn't quiet my interest in covered animal dishes. I still go around asking questions, looking for ones I don't have, picking up bargains and buying odd pieces. That is very satisfying to buy a top in one place and a matching bottom in another town.

Shortly thereafter, while we were setting up in a show in Indianapolis, Goldie was out picking the other booths and purchased two of the split-ribbed base animal dishes. When I noticed one of the dishes had a string attached to it which read "From the collection of Wallace Eaton, photographed for Millard's book," I went to the dealer for more information.

That day she had purchased the dish from Mrs. Luthe, a lady in a booth across the hall and gladly directed me to her. Mrs. Luthe had more covered animal dishes (some with the same note attached – which I purchased) and even more at home. I made an appointment to visit her home in Albion, Ilinois and purchased the remainder of the collection. She explained that she and her husband (before his death) had bought the collection from Mr. Wallace Eaton of Charleston. "Mr. Eaton of the Five Mile House?" I asked.

This unusual set of circumstances is how we became the proud owner of the majority of the covered animal dishes photographed for the book *Opaque Glass* by Dr. S.T. Millard.

I phoned Mr. Eaton shortly thereafter, but as he was getting up in years and not in good health, a lot of the questions I asked he could only reply that he did not remember. He did say he had packed the collection and shipped it to Kansas City to be photographed and only one piece got broken.

We were more careful with our collection. We hauled it to Paducah, carefully unwrapped and rewrapped it after it was photographed – constantly warning the photographer and the editor to be careful. Only one piece got broken and as you might guess, I did it. The boys were nice, but after all my warnings, they couldn't avoid their snickering.

And let me warn you – covered animal dishes break easily. The proper way to pick one up is to lift the lid with one hand to remove it and then when it is at least 2 feet out of reach, pick up the bottom piece with the other hand. There seems to be some kind of magnetism that draws them and they will clang together if this step is not followed. Never pick up both pieces at the same time. There seems to be something that makes the lid jump around and often breaks one or the other.

I have broken more covered animal dishes in the last few years than I have ever broken glass before in all the years that I have handled it, and Goldie agrees, "Age has got nothing to do with it."

All dishes pictured in Plates 1, 2 and 3 are the type first produced by McKee for use as food containers and were sold to packers in large lots. No records are known to exist that suggest they were ever sold in any other way.

There were 20 different tops – all fitting the same 5½" oval base. Some were marked "McKee," – most were not. All I have seen that were made by McKee are milk glass, with the exception of caramel slag or Greentown-type chocolate glass. Those not pictured are: cat, cow, doubleheaded chicken, frog, hen, lamb, pig, owl head and Baby Moses.

Some of the dishes have been reproduced by Joe St. Clair, Kemple, Degenhart and others. The problem is – how do you tell the difference. I have found nothing that works 100% of the time with the exception of the pieces marked "McKee." So, my advice to you is simply refuse to pay more than the least prices unless you are absolutely sure, but remember they are all collectible and will more than likely go up in price.

Plate 1. Left to right: hen with chicks, turkey, dove.

Plate 2. Left to right: swan, elephant, lion.

Plate 1

Plate 2

Plate 3. Left to right: squirrel, dog, rabbit.

Plate 4. McKee duck on left and pintail duck on the right by Kemple on split-rib base.

The one on the right appears to be a mismatch as this top was first produced by Westmoreland and the bottom by McKee, but I have reason to believe they were reproduced by Kemple and sold as they are here, as you will see in Plate 6.

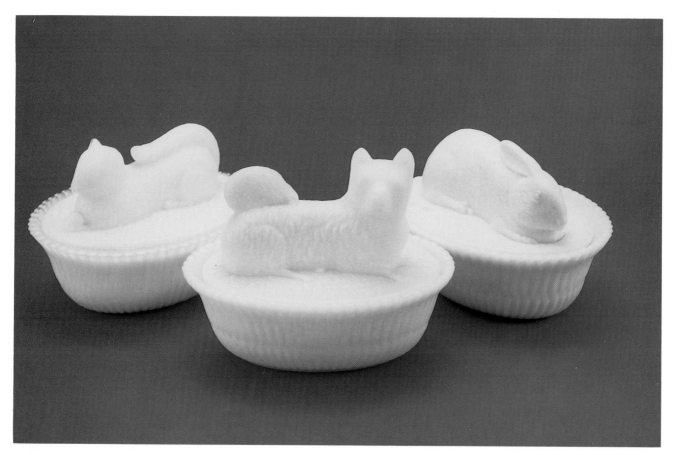

Plate 3

Plate 4

Plate 5. The horse on the left is not marked but believed to be McKee. The other horse is believed to be a reproduction – probably St. Clair.

Notice the position of the horse – especially its head. This in itself is not conclusive, but the fact is that the horse on the left came from a large collection that I purchased some time ago which contained nothing but good old dishes, and the horse on the right was purchased at a flea market where reproductions and out-right fakes were the rule rather than the exception. I can sometimes tell more about a piece knowing where it came from than any other way.

Plate 6. Blue pintail duck (top by Westmoreland) on Kemple split-rib base and domed rabbit on Kemple split-rib base.

Plate 5

Plate 6

Plate 7. Bust of Dewey on round base made by Indiana Tumbler & Goblet Co., Greentown, Indiana, (commonly called Greentown Glass).

Plate 8. Left to right: cat on tall hamper, dome rabbit, dolphin with serrated edge.

These are three of the famous Greentown covered animal dishes in chocolate glass. Although they were made in several different colors, none were reproduced in this form. That is with the exception of those made by the Summit Glass Company which were marked with a "V" in the bottom.

Plate 7

Plate 8

Plate 9. Reproduction of Greentown dolphin with sawtooth edge probably by Kemple. This piece has been reproduced by several companies in several colors but with notable differences. One advanced collector told me, "If it has 10 full teeth on each side and the tail is hollow past the curve or the fin, then it's Greentown regardless of color."

Plate 10. Serrated-edge Greentown dolphin and sawtooth-edge dolphin reproduction.

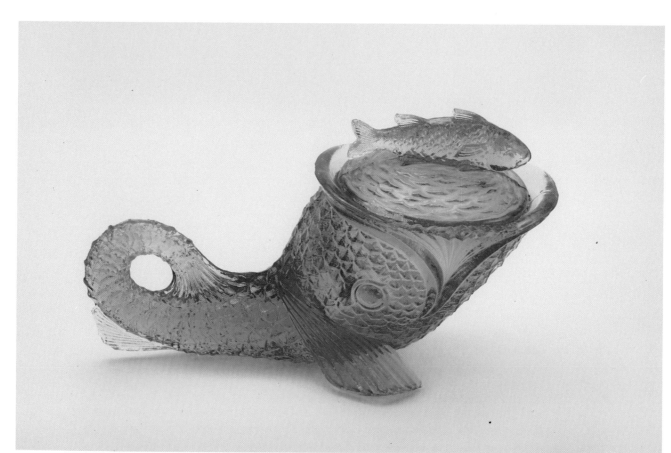

Plate 9

Plate 10

Plate 11. Greentown hen on diamond basketweave nest.

Plate 12. Close-up of eye. To me, this is the easiest of all to tell because of the eye. No other hen has this type eye. Others are slanted or oriental-type, whereas this one is perfectly round. It has not been reproduced.

Not pictured are fighting cocks, bird with berry on same diamond basketweave base and cat on low hamper which have not been reproduced. Also, not pictured are bird with berry on split-rib base (reproduced by Degenhart and St. Clair), bird with berry on a basketweave base (not diamond basketweave) which had been reproduced by Wright.

Plate 11

Plate 12

Items shown in the next five photographs were made by Westmoreland Specialty and Westmoreland Glass Company. They came in blue, white, blue head with white body, white head with blue body, and transparent amber. The color of the body determined the color of the base. These were all companion pieces. They are 5¼" long.

Plate 13. White rooster on wide-rib base and white hen on diamond basketweave base.

Plate 14. Blue rooster on wide-rib base and blue hen on diamond basketweave base.

Plate 15. White rooster with blue head on wide-rib base and hen with blue head on diamond basketweave base.

Plate 13

Plate 14

Plate 15

Plate 16. Rooster with blue body and white head on wide-rib base and blue hen with white head on diamond basketweave base.

Plate 17. Dog with white head and blue body on a blue wide-rib base and cat with a white head and blue body on a wide-rib base.

Plate 16

Plate 17

Plate 18. Quail top on a scroll base, maker unknown and white cat which is 5½" long. Same as in Plate 17.

Plate 19. The rooster on the left has an unusual color for goofus glass. The wide-rib base is white milk glass. The rooster on the right is dark opaque blue. Attributed to Westmoreland.

Plate 20. The duck on the left is 5½" long. It has a cattail base. Maker unknown. The pintail duck on the right has a diamond basketweave base. It was first produced by the Westmoreland Specialty Company and is 5½" long. It also came with a white head and blue body and base and vice versa.

Plate 18

Plate 19

Plate 20

Plate 21. The hen on the left is a new or recent color. It has a wide-rib base. The amber sheep on the right has a split-rib base. It is also recent.

Plate 22. The hen on the left is on a cattail base. It is 5½" long. Maker unknown. The hen on the right is on a basketweave base with woven edges, made by Vallerysthal. It is 5⅝" long. Maker unknown.

Plate 21

Plate 22

The lamb, rabbit and lion on picket base in the usual colors of blue and white and the combinations of blue and white were products of the Westmoreland Specialty Company. The white rabbit has been heavily reproduced by Westmoreland Glass. Some are marked WG. Rabbits are now also being imported from Taiwan.

Plate 23. The lamb on the left is on a picket base. The lion on the right is also on the picket base.

Plate 24. Left to right: Two mule-eared rabbits on picket base, one with pink ears and eyes, lamb with white head and blue body and base. Picket base has smooth top, probably ground.

Plate 23

Plate 24

Plate 25. Straight headed hen in two sizes smaller made by Imperial Glass although it is not marked. The larger is early Indiana glass before the beaded edge was added.

Plate 26. Straight headed hen in white milk glass and blue carnival. Indiana Glass Company. White milk glass bottom is the latest type used.

Plate 25

Plate 26

Plate 27. Straight headed hen in marigold carnival and amber. This straight headed hen is still being produced by Indiana Glass Company.

Plate 28. The one on the left is a Hazel Atlas little hen. This little hen was produced by this company for many years. Some were marked, but most were not. The hen on the right has chicks on basketweave base. This is a medium size hen of heavy glass resting on a shallow base. It is believed to have been made by Smith because it comes in many different colors.

Plate 27

Plate 28

Plate 29. Amberina hen and a rooster. Both are on Vallerysthal type bases. The rooster top is the McKee straight back rooster type. Both are L.G. Wright productions.

Plate 30. The Atterbury duck. Dated, reproduced by Fenton with F mark.

The authentic Atterbury duck always had a "Patent Apld for" or "Patd March 15 1887" embossed on the bottom of the base. They were 11" long. They were found white, white with blue head, white with amethyst head, all blue, and all amethyst.

Plate 31. Reproductions by Wright of the Atterbury duck.

Both Wright and Imperial reproduced the Atterbury duck in all of the original colors and combinations plus some of their own. The Wright reproductions are unmarked. The Imperial pieces not only have the original date, but also the "IG" has been added.

Plate 29

Plate 30

Plate 31

Plate 32. Ribbed fox on lacy Atterbury base, 6¼" long. Ribbed lion on lace Atterbury base, 6¼".

Plate 33. Ribbed fox on ribbed base.

Plate 34. Ribbed lion on ribbed base.

The foxes and the lions are interchangeable as are the bases of the Atterbury hen and rooster of the same size so any combination may be found. The original lion was dated Aug 6, 1889 inside the lid. Both Westmoreland and Imperial reproduced the lion and the fox. The Imperial reproductions have the "IG" inside the head. The fox was reproduced by Kemple and Westmoreland. Some of the Westmoreland's were marked. The original had sockets for glass eyes so all with molded eyes are believed to be reproductions.

Plate 32

Plate 33

Plate 34

Plate 35. Entwined fish by Atterbury. This lid is marked August 6, 1889. It also fits the compote pictured in Plate 42. It is 6" diameter.

Plate 36. Hand and dove. Originally by Atterbury. Lid dated August 27, 1889. Reproduced by Westmoreland without date and "WG" on bottom of base. These could be interchanged.

Plate 35

Plate 36

Plate 37. Cat on lacy base. Originally by Atterbury. Lid dated August 6, 1889. Reproduced by Westmoreland without date and "WG" on bottom of base.

Plate 38. Atterbury hen on lacy base. Made by Atterbury in a variety of colors combined with white. White with light blue head, white with dark blue head, transparent blue head, transparent purple head. Red marbled back, blue marbled back, orange marbled back, green marbled back, purple marbled back and mixed (several colors) marbled back. Occasionally a marbled back hen may be found on a matching marbled Atterbury basketweave base. They are rare.

Plate 37

Plate 38

Plate 39. Raised-wing swan. Attributed to Atterbury. Reproduced by Westmoreland with molded eyes. The originals had sockets for glass eyes. The bottom of the lid is about ¼" thick. Another variety was produced with the bottom of the lid hollow and about 1" tall. It has not been reproduced.

Plate 40. Challinor, Taylor & Co. rooster on Atterbury lacy and basketweave base.

Plate 39

Plate 40

Plate 41. Boar's head. Atterbury patent date May 29, 1888, appears on both the bottom and top. It is found in blue as well as white and it is 9½" long.

Plate 42. Chick and eggs on round compote or base. First produced by Atterbury, the patent date August 6, 1889 is found on the underside of the lid on the original. Reproduced without the date by Westmoreland, some are marked "WG." The compote has been reproduced by Westmoreland; the vertical column in the center of the stand is left out of the reproductions.

Plate 43. Large Atterbury rabbit. The patent date Aug. 6, 1889, appears on the bottom of this 9" dish. Also found in the 6" size and also in blue. Reproduced by Imperial with "IG" on bottom in addition to patent date.

Not pictured is steer's head covered dish made by Challinor, Taylor & Co., 7½" long.

Plate 41

Plate 42

Plate 43

Plate 44. Uncle Tom cigar holder. I purchased this one at Five Mile House auction. The hat is made of wood. It is pictured on Plate 295 in Millard's book without the hat. I recently saw a picture of Uncle Tom with a milk glass hat.

Plate 45. Large rooster on Westmoreland base. Notice difference in detail of these basketweave bases.

Plate 46. Showing difference in shades of blue Atterbury hen heads.

Plate 44

Plate 45

Plate 46

Plate 47. Largest and smallest in our collection. 8" Fenton hen and 1" hen marked "Vallerysthal."

Plate 48. The Pekinese dog on the left is attributed to Sandwich, 4-3/4". The setter on the right is on a square base with much detail, gun hunting bag, etc. Attributed to Vallerysthal.

Plate 47

Plate 48

Plate 49. The British lion on the left is an easy one to detect because "The British Lion" is embossed across the base. Maker unknown, 6¼" long. The lion on the right has a scroll base. Maker unknown, 5½" long.

Plate 50. The standing rooster is attributed to L.E. Smith. A slightly different version was produced by Westmoreland. Later reproduced in many colors by Westmoreland Glass Company. Some are marked. The large hen, Challinor, Taylor & Co. styled lid with a Vallerysthal-type base, was reproduced in this combination in many colors by Wright.

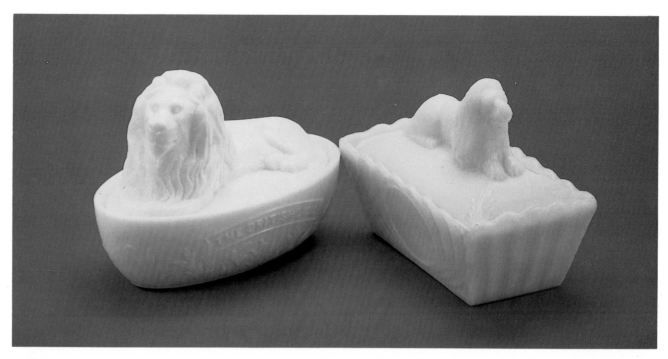

Plate 49

Plate 50

Plate 51. **The hen on a sleigh and the chick in an egg on a sleigh were originally by Westmoreland Specialty but was reproduced by Westmoreland Glass, 5½" long. They have been reproduced in other colors. The circles or dots on the sleigh supports are missing.**

Not pictured is the Santa Claus on sleigh which is the same as above. Also the small hen on two-handled basket and chick in egg on two-handled basket.

Tops to the last five items mentioned are interchangeable. They are all attributed to Westmoreland Specialty, later reproduced by Westmoreland Glass. I have never seen the Santa Claus on basket base.

Also not pictured is a robed Santa Claus on sleigh. This one is slightly smaller than the one above and tops are not interchangeable. Also there are two supports and the sleigh is not scrolled.

Plate 52. **Left, chick on top of vertical egg, maker unknown, probably very late, 6½" high. Right, chick in vertical egg, maker unknown, 6½" high. Also comes in small 3¾" size.**

Plate 51

Plate 52

Plates 53, 54 & 55. Wavy base duck first produced by Challinor, Taylor & Co. in white variegated blue and variegated green. Later produced by its successor, U.S. Glass, in white only and then reproduced in satinized transparent blue by Fenton and in a variety of colors by Westmoreland, 8" long.

Not pictured is the dominecker duck. This duck is same as above except it is decorated with fired-on paint maybe intended to look like the mallard duck but the colors more closely resemble those of the dominecker chickens.

Plate 53

Plate 54

Plate 55

Plate 56. Block swan. This one was produced only by Challinor, Taylor & Co. in white and clear frosted – plus the variegated blue and green and by its successor, The U.S. Glass Co. in white only, 7" long.

Not pictured is the block swan top also found in combination with the basketweave base by the same company in all of the above colors.

Plate 57. Mother eagle. This one is the same as above except it has been reproduced by Westmoreland in several colors. All that I have seen are marked. The two pictured here are marked "WG." Recently reissued by Fenton with F mark.

Plate 56

Plate 57

Plate 58. Rooster and hen by Challinor, Taylor & Co., 8".

Not pictured are a dominecker rooster and hen with all over fired-on paint to resemble dominecker chickens.

Plate 59. Challinor, Taylor & Co. rooster clear with paint, 8". Reproduction hen by Wright.

Plate 58

Plate 59

Plate 60. Closed-neck swan by Westmoreland Specialty Company. The white one was purchased at the Five Mile House auction. The top is pictured in Plate 278 of Millard's book but it is on the wrong split-rib base. It is my guess that they were mixed by the photographer when they were unpacked as was the straight-back rooster in Plate 276 on opposite page and two-headed chicken in Plate 234.

Plate 61. Vallerysthal swan. Both bottoms are marked. This has recently been reproduced in Taiwan in several colors. 5½" long.

Plate 60

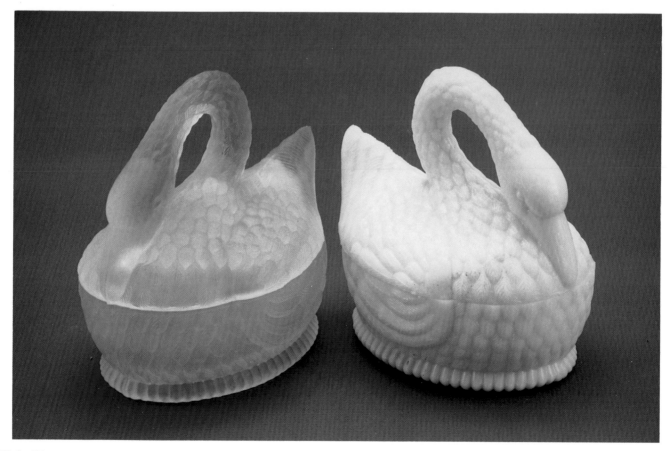

Plate 61

Plate 62. The swimming duck by Vallerysthal was made in two sizes (5" & 5¾") and in several colors.

Plate 63. This label is affixed to the bottom of the yellow duck in the preceding plate.

Plate 62

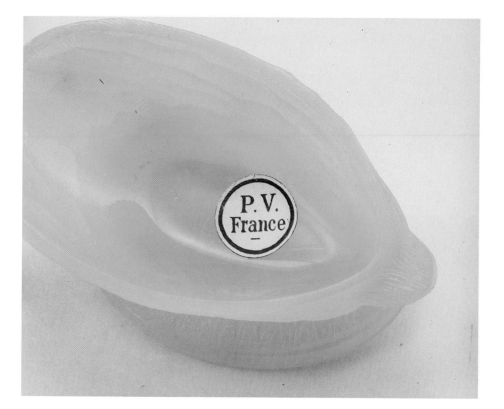

Plate 63

Plate 64. Robin on pedestal base made by Vallerysthal recently reproduced by Westmoreland in many colors.

Plate 65. Breakfast set by Vallerysthal.

Plate 64

Plate 65

Plate 66. Fancy dish with squirrel atop lid, attributed to Vallerysthal. Double washtub with boy washing dog on top of lid, "Puppy Love," attributed to Dermay.

Plate 67. Rat on large egg. Vallerysthal, also made in white. This one was purchased at Five Mile House auction. It is also pictured in *Schroeder's Antiques Price Guide, 6th Edition*.

Not pictured is a dish of this type with a rabbit atop an egg. I have seen this in two sizes in white only.

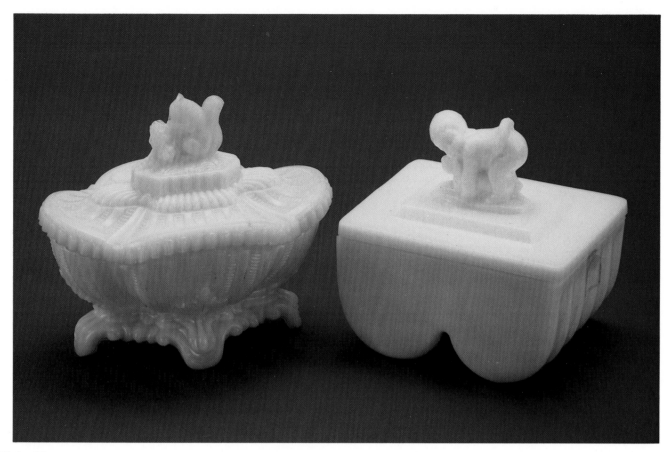

Plate 66

Plate 67

Plate 68. Bird on round basketweave base. Vallerysthal. Reproduced extensively in many colors. Robin on nest once thought to be Greentown – now disclaimed by most Greentown collectors, maker unknown, 6½" tall.

Plate 69. Vallerysthal rabbit usually marked, clear white and blue. Jack rabbit attributed to Flaccus, clear and white.

Plate 68

Plate 69

Plate 70. Fish on collared base, Central Glass Co. Elephant with rider by Vallerysthal, 7" long. Also found in white and blue.

Plate 71. Flat fish on ribbed base, attributed to Fostoria, 8½" long. Snail on strawberry, Vallerysthal, 5¼" tall.

Plate 70

Plate 71

Plate 72. Flat fish in transparent green.

Plate 73. Chick on eggs on tall two-handled basket base. Frosted transparent blue glass which has been painted, maker unknown.

Plate 72

Plate 73

Plate 74. Horseshoe butter dish, Aetna Glass Co. Elephant standing, 9" long, Co-operative Flint Glass Co. and Indiana Glass, now Taiwan.

Plate 75. Rabbit on the left is on a 8" basketweave base, U.S. Glass, reproduced by Westmoreland, Imperial, and Fenton. The rabbit on the right, by Cambridge Glass, also came in a 4" size.

Plate 74

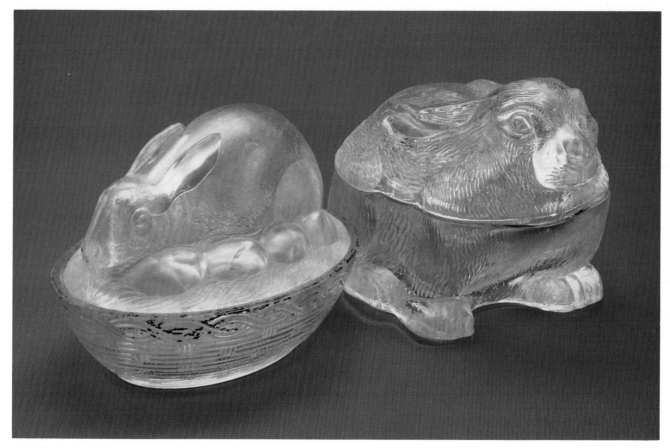

Plate 75

Plate 76. Crystal swan, maker unknown, recent. This certainly is not a covered "animal" dish but it fits well in this collection as several pictured hereafter. Conestoga wagon, L.E. Smith Glass Co.

Plate 77. Turtle pictured in Millard's book in white glass, maker unknown. Knobby-back turtle, originally made by Vallerysthal, has been reproduced by L.G. Wright Co.

Plate 76

Plate 77

Plate 78. Dolphin on sauce dish attributed to Westmoreland, 7¼" long. Fish on shiff, maker unknown, 7½" long.

Plate 79. Turtle on scroll base with two handles, maker unknown, 7½" long. Resting camel believed to be early Westmoreland Specialty Company, 6¼". Crawfish on same scroll base as turtle, 7¼" long, maker unknown. I have seen the resting camel recently in a dark transparent blue believed to be new.

Not pictured is a resting water buffalo which reminds me of the resting camel, probably Vallerysthal.

Plate 78

Plate 79

Plate 80. Left, amber dog on wide rib base, Westmoreland. Right, amber swan on knobby basketweave base. "Patent appl'd for" appears inside the top attributed to Belmont Glass Works, 7" long. This was bought at Five Mile House auction.

Plate 81. Chicks in oblong basket, 2¼" x 4¼", maker unknown. Chicks on round basket, chicks emerging from shell on round two-handled basket, maker unknown.

Plate 80

Plate 81

Plate 82. Baby Moses on cattail or reed base, maker unknown, 6¼".

Plate 83. Rabbit on wheat base, deer on fallen tree base and hen on chick base. These are Flaccus pieces although they are not always marked as such. They were not manufactured by Flaccus but were used as condiment containers by the company. They were probably commissioned by Flaccus to one or more glass houses for the Flaccus Company's use.

Not pictured are beaver on bee and flower base, lamb on Bo Peep base, dog on wheat base, baboon on fleur-de-lis base, frog on reed base, monkey on arrow and scroll base and dining pig. Although the six not pictured are generally accepted as Flaccus, it has not been proven – with the exception of the lamb, which is sometimes marked.

Plate 82

Plate 83

Plate 84. Rabbit emerging from horizontal egg, two pieces, maker unknown. Chick emerging from horizontal egg, two pieces, attributed to Dithridge Co.

Plate 85. Small turkey marked "I.G." We think of Imperial as the reproducer. In that case, who was the original producer of this small turkey? Ribbed rooster on lacy base – we know this is a reproduction of the Atterbury lacy base, but what about the top? It reminds us of the ribbed fox and lion that also fits this base. Is it also a reproduction of an Atterbury product? Was there also a ribbed hen? I still have more questions than answers. Both pieces are marked "IG."

Plate 84

Plate 85

Plate 86. Monkey top as listed on page 80. Hen top, amber with white head. Westmoreland Specialty.

Plate 87. Bird on jar marked "Avon" on bottom. Standing turkey made by L.E. Smith. Small hen, Westmoreland, 3" is recent.

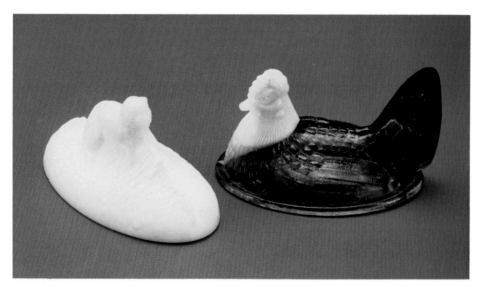

Plate 86

Plate 87

Plate 88. Swan creamer and sugar bowl, also came in blue. Maker Westmoreland. Reproduced by Summit Art Glass in many colors.

Plate 89. Large standing turkey, U.S. Glass. Small standing turkey made by L.E. Smith.

Plate 88

Plate 89

Plate 90. **The American Hen is one of several novelty pieces pertaining to the Spanish American War, base marked "Pat. Applied for." Attributed to Eagle Glass reportedly reproduced but by whom and when, we have been unable to find out. Cannon on drum is another Spanish American War novelty, made by Vallerysthal.**

Not pictured is cannon on kettle drum.

Plate 91. **"Remember the Maine," green.**

Plate 92. **"Remember the Maine" in clear. These have been recently reproduced. I have seen them for sale in dark transparent blue and have been told they are also available in green. The reproductions do not have stars above the shield on front of the boat base.**

Plate 90

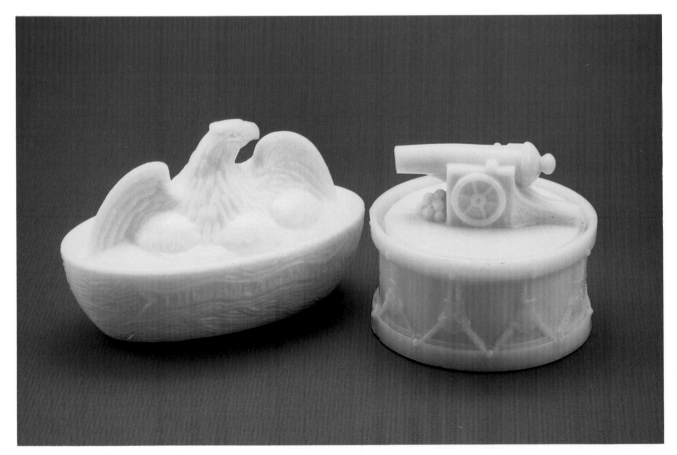

Plate 91

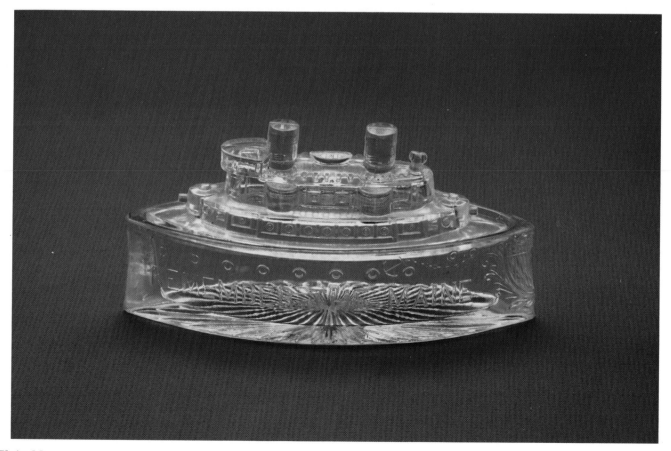

Plate 92

Plate 93. "Uncle Sam on Battleship" attributed to Flaccus, another Spanish American War novelty, 6⅝" long.

Plate 94. "Uncle Sam on Battleship" in opaque blue. This color first showed up on the market about 10 years ago. Undoubtedly it is a reproduction but from where, we don't know. Note no detail at all on face.

Plate 95. Dewey on tile base attributed to Flaccus, 6⅝".

Not pictured is Dewey on a Patriotic base, same as above except base shows an American shield with crossed cannons over the word "cavite" on one side and "manila" on the other.

Plate 93

Plate 94

Plate 95

Plate 96. Battleship Oregon. This could be the Wheeling, Olympia or Oregon – the difference is the name embossed on the side, attributed to Flaccus, 6⅜" long. Battleship Newark – Warman's Milk glass addenda show this in Plate 18B with Flaccus paper label still attached. The other one is the "Man o' War."

Plate 97. Battleship Maine easily recognized by the word "Maine" on the fore deck, 7¾", maker unknown, but the one on the left shows a light purple cast thought to be Atterbury.

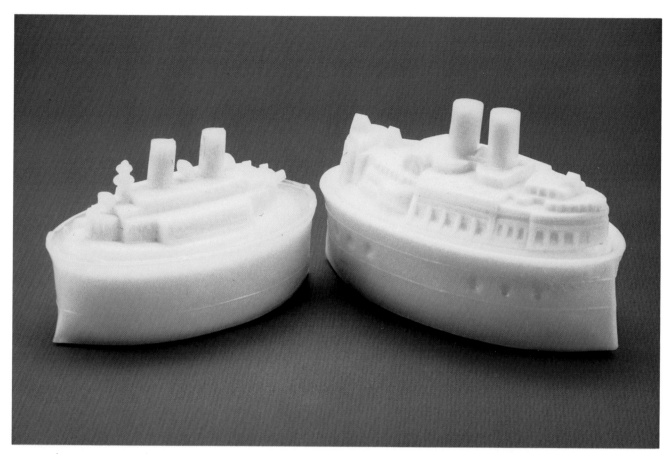

Plate 96

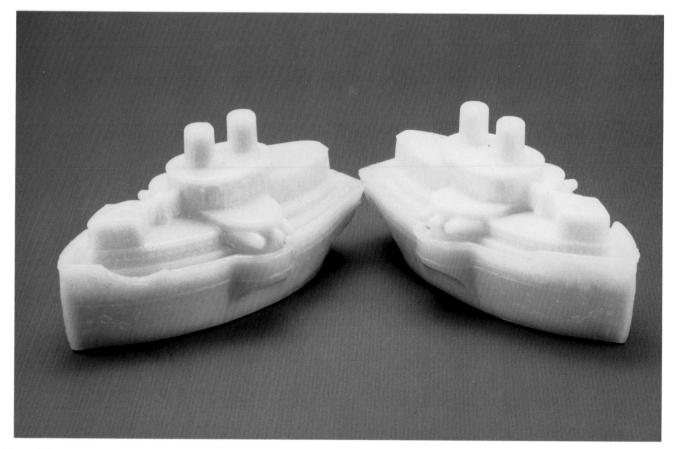

Plate 97

Plate 98. Brick schoolhouse, Westmoreland Specialty, container for mustard, also for bank, 3¾" high. Fainting couch, early novelty, maker unknown, 5" long. Log cabin, Westmoreland Specialty, mustard container and bank, 3¾" high.

Plate 99. Bottom of log cabin pictured in Plate 98.

Plate 98

Plate 99

Plate 100. Cinderella's coach, by L.E. Smith, 5¼" long. Football, recent, maker unknown. Baseball, recent, Fire-King. We also have a Fire-King golf ball not pictured.

Plate 101. Large fish attributed to Challinor, Taylor & Co.

Plate 100

Plate 101

Plate 102. Sad iron butter dish, probably Depression Era, maker unknown. Cookstove covered dish with sad iron finial, maybe same era, maker unknown. Both pieces reproduced by L.G. Wright.

Plate 103. Figural donkey and elephant powder jars. Probably Jeannette Glass Depression Era. Lovebirds, recent, could be Westmoreland.

Plate 104. Swan powder jar, Jeannette Glass, late 1960's.

Plate 102

Plate 103

Plate 104

Plate 107. Duck soap dish, clear and carnival with painted bill, Depression Era.

Plate 108. Old Abe jar 6½", high, maker unknown, and because it was there – we picture the owl fruit jar with eagle insert. Top 6¼" high, maker unknown.

Plate 107

Plate 108

Plate 109. Bull's head mustard jar by Atterbury. The tongue (ladle) is missing and the right horn is broken off but it is a good example of opalescent found in some old milk glass. "Pat. appli. for" appears on bottom of the original, reproductions are not marked.

Plate 110. Bull's head mustard jar reproduced by L.G. Wright in purple slag without "pat. applied for" on bottom nor (ladle) tongue.

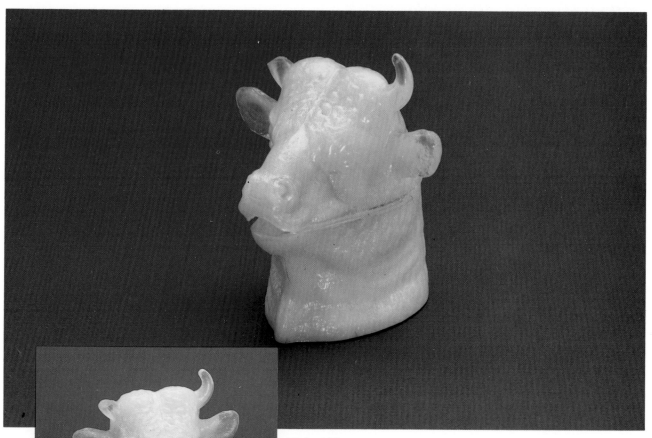

Plate 109

Plate 110

Plate 111. Recent reproductions of the Vallerysthal swan, Westmoreland lovebirds and Vallerysthal bird on round basketweave base. These are pretty and could increase in value in the future.

Plate 112. But what have we here? An "H" inside a diamond. Is this a mark of the manufacturer? No, I suggest it was placed here solely for the purpose of aiding fraud.

This mark does not appear on all of these dishes nor even all of the same type. As I said before, they are pretty but it is the purpose for which they were intended that turns me off. They are pictured here for the sole purpose of making you aware of the pitfalls of collecting; but if you feel you must have one of them for your collection, please don't pay over gift shop price.

Plate 111

Plate 112

Plate 113-118. The remaining items pictured were purchased indirectly from the largest supplier of merchandise to the crooked auctioneers, the crooked flea marketer and the crooked antique dealers in the nation. How much longer is the American collector going to let these mongrels operate – though they have operated barely inside the law for years. In years past, they would have been tarred and feathered and ridden out of town on a rail. Don't ask me who they are. Ask the young lady in Kansas City who paid $45.00 for one of these swans because the auctioneer said it might be Heisey, and the nice old lady in New Mexico who bought one because the antique dealer said, "I don't know," and the 10,000 or more other people who have been duped. Yes, I once purchased a toothpick holder for $35.00 and later discovered I could have bought a dozen like it for $36.00, but most of you know who they are anyway.

Plate 113

Plate 114

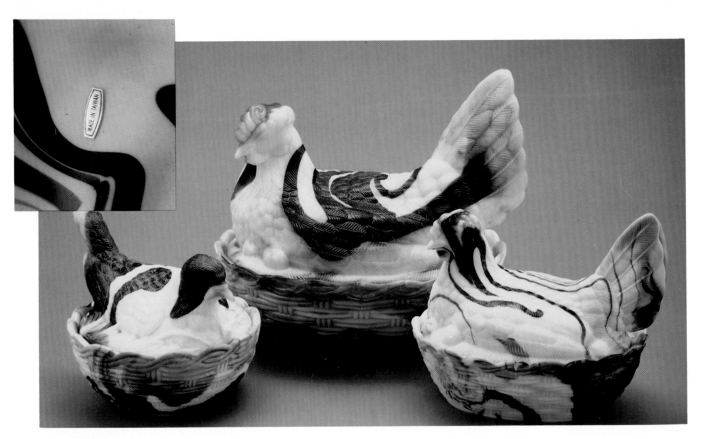

Plate 115

Plate 116

Plate 117

Plate 118

I now have in my possession seven catalogs dating from 1962 through 1972 from the Westmoreland Glass Company. Listed below are the covered animal dishes shown in them.

Plate 13.
Small rooster, 5½", wide ribbed base – white.

Ribbed fox on diamond basketweave base – white and purple marble.

Ribbed fox on basketweave base – white.

Plate 17.
Cat on wide rib base – purple marble mixed color marble.

Plate 24.
Mule-eared rabbit – white, white with pink ears, pink.

Plate 32.
Lion on lacy base – white.

Rabbit on lacy base – white.

Plate 37.
Cat on lacy base – white, green marble.

Plate 39.
Raised-wing swan – white, frosty blue.

Plate 40.
Rooster on lacy base – white.

Plate 45.
Rooster and almond basketweave base, 6½" – white, purple and green marble.

Plate 47.
Hen on basketweave base, 2" – opaque green, white, opaque yellow, opaque blue and opaque red.

Mother eagle on lacy base – white.

Plate 50.
Standing rooster – amber, transparent green, transparent blue, white and purple marble.

Medium hen on diamond basketweave base, 6½" – amber, transparent green, transparent blue, white, purple and green marble, almond, opaque yellow.

Small hen on diamond basketweave base, 5½", amber, transparent green, transparent blue, white, olive green, purple and green marble, chartreuse.

Plate 53.
Wavy base duck – white, white with antique gold, opaque blue, clear frosted,

blue frosted, yellow marble, opaque mint green.

Plate 57.
Mother eagle basketweave base – white.

Plate 64.
Robin on pedestal nest – amber, transparent green, transparent blue, white, frosted blue, olive green, frosted green and apricot, chartreuse, mother-of-pearl, almond, frosty pink and yellow marble.

Plate 75.
Rabbit on diamond basketweave – white.

Plate 79.
Resting camel – frosty amber.

Plate 87.
Hen on basketweave base – white, frosted amber, blue and green.

Plate 103.
Lovebirds – white, amber, transparent blue, transparent green, olive green, frosty green, blue and apricot. Purple marble, chartreuse, opaque blue, mint green and almond.

Now, I do not mean that this is all that has been reproduced in this time period, but I have seen these listed in these catalogs. I am sure the list is incomplete.

In the 1967 catalog, a statement was made that due to numerous instances having been observed in which a new product was sold as old and at a high price, they had established a policy of stamping "WG" on some of their products. To this, Mr. Brainard, we say "thank you." But since hindsight is always 20/20, could this be a case of too little – too late?

Value Guide

I called on several of my dealer and collector friends, who are much more knowledgeable than I, for help in putting this value guide together. Most were willing to help, but none would agree to accept either the credit or the blame for it. I found that in most cases the values received from the west were higher than those from the east. Since certain pieces had higher values, I tried to use an average quoted value where possible.

Key: * One Piece Marked   **Both Pieces Marked

McKee 5½" Condiment Containers Unmarked

Plate 1
Hen w/chicks $165.00
* $265.00
** $275.00
Turkey......................$110.00
......................$220.00
** $250.00
Dove $125.00
* $245.00
** $250.00

Plate 2
Swan......................$220.00
* $250.00
** $250.00
Elephant................$1,300.00
* $1,500.00
Lion $185.00
* $245.00
** $300.00

Plate 3
Squirrel $185.00
* $245.00
** $325.00
Dog (chow)................$275.00
* $375.00
** $500.00
Rabbit $175.00
* $250.00
** $300.00

Not Pictured
Cat......................$175.00
* $275.00
** $300.00
Cow $825.00
* $950.00
** $550.00
Double-headed
    chicken................$450.00
* $550.00
** $750.00
Frog $550.00
* $1,000.00
Hen......................$200.00
* $350.00

** $175.00
Lamb $185.00
* $220.00
** $245.00
Pig......................$1,000.00
* $1,100.00
** $1,200.00
Owl Head $575.00
* $750.00
** $850.00
Baby Moses $750.00
* $850.00
** $1,000.00

Plate 4
McKee Duck $185.00
* $250.00
** $350.00
Pintail Duck reproduction
    (white)......................$65.00
    (colored) $75.00

Plate 5
Horse on left $185.00
* $220.00
** $275.00
Reproduced Horse
    (white)......................$75.00
    (colored) $30.00

Plate 6
Blue Pin Tail Duck $60.00
White Domed Rabbit
    (reproduction) $50.00

Greentown Glass
Plate 7
Dewey Bust, white $350.00
    transparent, clear
        or colored $100.00

Plate 8
Cat on hamper, white..$400.00
    transparent, clear
        or colored $300.00
    chocolate $400.00
    nile green $1,200.00

Domed Rabbit, white....$75.00
    transparent, clear
        or colored $185.00
    chocolate $500.00
Dolphin serrated rim
    transparent, clear
        or colored $375.00
    chocolate $400.00
    nile green..........$2,000.00
    golden agate $875.00

Plate 9
Dolphin Sawtooth rim
    white......................$525.00
    transparent, clear
        or colored $475.00
    chocolate $250.00

**Reproductions by
Kemple or St. Clair**
Plate 10
Dolphin Sawtooth
    white......................$75.00
    transparent, clear
        or colored $45.00
    chocolate $65.00

Plate 11
Hen, white..................$250.00
    transparent, clear
        or colored $300.00
    chocolate $675.00
    nile green............$1,200.00
    golden agate $1,400.00
Not Pictured:
Fighting Cocks,
    white..................$1,200.00
    transparent, clear
        or colored $850.00
    chocolate $1,725.00
    nile green............$2,000.00
Bird w/Berry, white $300.00
    transparent, clear
        or colored $300.00
    chocolate $900.00
    nile green............$2,000.00

Cat on low hamper,
   transparent, clear
     or colored $300.00
   chocolate $575.00
Bird w/Berry on split rib
   base, chocolate......$250.00
   Repros any color $25.00

Westmoreland Specialty
Plate 13
Rooster, white $40.00
   other colors.............$95.00
Hen, white...................$35.00
   other colors.............$85.00

Plate 14
Blue Rooster.................$65.00
Blue Hen $55.00

Plate 15
White Rooster w/blue
   head $70.00
White Hen w/blue
   head $65.00

Plate 16
Blue Rooster w/white
   head $70.00
Blue Hen w/white
   head $65.00

Plate 17
Dog, white...................$50.00
   blue $60.00
   white w/blue head....$65.00
   blue w/white head....$65.00
Cat, white...................$50.00
   blue $60.00
   white w/blue head....$65.00
   blue w/white head....$65.00

Miscellaneous
Plate 18
Quail..........................$65.00
White Cat $40.00

Plate 19
Rooster Goofus $65.00
Blue Opaque Rooster....$90.00

Plate 20
Duck on cattail base.....$85.00
Pintail Duck, white........$55.00
   blue $75.00

white w/blue head..$125.00
blue w/white head..$135.00
Plate 21
Hen on wide rib base....$45.00
Lamb on split rib base..$45.00

Plate 22
Hen on cattail base.......$85.00
Hen on basketweave,
   white.....................$135.00
   other colors...........$165.00

Plate 23
Lamb on picket base,
   white.......................$95.00
   blue $125.00
   white w/blue head..$100.00
   blue w/white head..$100.00
Lion on picket base,
   white.......................$95.00
   blue $125.00
   white w/blue head..$100.00
   blue w/white head..$100.00

Plate 24
Mule eared rabbits (still being
   reproduced),
   white.......................$40.00
   blue $55.00
   white w/blue head..$100.00
   blue w/white head..$100.00
   other colors.............$60.00

Plate 25
Straight Headed Hen,
   clear.......................$15.00
   color $30.00

Plate 26 & 27
Straight Headed Hen,
   white.......................$15.00
   carnival $25.00
   clear.......................$15.00
   other.......................$15.00

Plate 28
Hazel Atlas Little Hen,
   marked $15.00
   unmarked $10.00
Hen w/Chicks,
   all colors $35.00

Plate 29
Hen, amberina $25.00
   other......................$20.00
Rooster, amberina $25.00
   other......................$20.00

Plate 30
Atterbury Duck, white.$245.00
   blue $850.00
   white w/blue head..$650.00
   white w/ amethyst
     head $300.00

Plate 31
Reproduced Atterbury Duck
   all colors $40.00

Plate 32
Ribbed Fox on lacy
   base, white dated ...$175.00
   no date $100.00
   IG $125.00
   WG........................$100.00
Ribbed Lion on lacy
   base, white dated ...$175.00
   no date $100.00
   IG $125.00
   WG........................$100.00

Plate 33
Ribbed Fox on rib
   base, white dated ...$175.00
Ribbed Lion on ribbed
   base, white dated ...$175.00

Plate 35
Entwined Fish, white on
   lacy base.................$170.00
   on compote $200.00

Plate 36
Hand & Dove, dated...$125.00
   no date $110.00
   marked WG $110.00

Plate 37
Cat on lacy base,
   dated $160.00
   no date $130.00
   WG white $130.00
   WG colored $150.00

Plate 38
Hen on lacy base,
   white.....................$120.00
   opaque blue head ..$225.00
   transparent blue.....$275.00
   amethyst head........$295.00
Marbled back, blue.....$300.00
   green $325.00
   red........................$325.00
   orange $300.00
   purple $200.00

mixed colors $375.00

Plate 39
Raised Wing Swan,
white....................$225.00
w/molded eyes........$85.00
shag or black..........$200.00
marked F................$50.00

Plate 40
Rooster, lacy white
base....................$75.00
basketweave base $65.00

Plate 41
Boar's Head, white ..$1,250.00
blue, rare $4,500.00
Not Pictured
Steer's head...........$2,750.00

Plate 42
Chick on eggs, dated ..$250.00
WG.........................$125.00
dated on compote ..$225.00
WG.........................$175.00

Plate 43
Atterbury Rabbit,
large white $300.00
large, blue..............$375.00
small, white............$225.00
small, blue $325.00
IG $85.00

Plate 44
Uncle Tom Cigar Holder
w/milk glass hat $500.00
wooden hat............$165.00
no hat $95.00

Plate 45
Large Rooster, white ...$110.00
opaque blue...........$125.00

Plate 47
Hen, 8" $150.00
Hen, 2" $20.00

Plate 48
Pekinese Dog, white ...$325.00
Setter, opaque blue $225.00
green $225.00
clear $150.00
other.....................$195.00

Plate 49
British Lion................$195.00

Lion on scroll base $75.00

Plate 50
Standing Rooster,
clear....................$45.00
Large Hen, frosted.......$75.00

Plate 51
Hen on sleigh, white.....$85.00
Chick in egg on sleigh...$95.00
Not Pictured
Santa Claus on sleigh .$100.00
Hen on basket.............$50.00
Chick in egg on
basket.....................$75.00
Robed Santa on
sleigh $175.00

Plate 52
Chick on top of egg $65.00
Chick in vertical egg,
white, small.............$75.00
white, large $120.00

Plates 53, 54, 55
Wavy Base Duck,
white.....................$125.00
blue $210.00
clear......................$65.00
white WG $65.00
other WG.................$75.00
Not Pictured
Dominecker Duck, painted
on white.................$275.00

Plate 56
Block Swan, white $300.00
clear frosted..........$145.00
variegated green.....$650.00
Not Pictured
Block Swan top on basket-
weave base, white ..$200.00
clear frosted..........$120.00

Plate 57
Mother Eagle, white $550.00
white WG $100.00
other WG...............$125.00

Plate 58
Large Rooster, white ...$135.00
Large Hen, white $110.00
Not Pictured
Dominecker Duck,
painted $200.00
Dominecker Rooster,
painted $150.00

Dominecker Hen,
painted $150.00

Plate 59
Large Rooster, clear
painted $95.00
Large Hen, blue w/white
head $85.00

Plate 60
Closed Neck Swan,
white.......................$75.00
blue $110.00

Plate 61
Vallerysthal Swan marked,
white.......................$95.00
clear frosted.............$65.00
other.......................$125.00

Plate 62
Swimming Duck,
white.......................$75.00
blue $100.00
other.......................$120.00

Plate 64
Robin on pedestal base marked,
white.......................$75.00
blue $90.00
other.......................$65.00
marked WG $35.00

Plate 65
Breakfast Set, white....$400.00
amber $450
blue $500

Plate 66
Squirrel Finial, white.....$95.00
blue $110.00
Puppy Love, white $200.00

Plate 67
Rat on egg, white........$225.00
pink $175.00
Not Pictured
Rabbit on egg
white.......................$225.00
blue $225.00

Plate 68
Bird on round basket marked,
white.......................$95.00
other.......................$75.00

not marked $25.00
Robin on nest, white...$200.00

Plate 69
Vallerysthal Rabbit, marked,
    white.....................$150.00
    clear.........................$95.00
    other.........................$95.00
    not marked $45.00
Jack Rabbit, white $200.00
    clear $150.00

Plate 70
Fish, clear frosted.......$150.00
Elephant w/rider,
    white $400.00
    blue $500.00
    clear frosted $200.00
    other $350.00

Plate 71 & 72
Fish, white.................$165.00
    blue $165.00
    clear.......................$45.00
    transparent green $75.00
Snail, white, large.......$120.00
    small......................$90.00

Plate 73
Chick on eggs frosted
    transparent blue.....$100.00

Plate 74
Horse Shoe Butter Dish,
    clear........................$45.00
Elephant, white $140.00
    black.....................$130.00
    clear........................$25.00
    Ritz blue................$140.00

Plate 75
Rabbit on basketweave
    base, white...............$95.00
    clear........................$65.00
Large Rabbit, clear $85.00
Small Rabbit, clear $95.00

Plate 76
Crystal Swan, clear $10.00
Covered Wagon, white ..$80.00
    clear........................$35.00

Plate 77
Large Turtle, white......$100.00
    amber.....................$45.00
    clear........................$35.00

Plate 78
Dolphin on sauce dish,
    white....................$100.00
    amber $45.00
    transparent blue.......$35.00
Fish on skiff, white $75.00

Plate 79
Turtle, white $185.00
Resting Camel, white ..$120.00
    opaque blue...........$150.00
Crawfish, white...........$185.00
Not Pictured
Resting water buffalo,
    white....................$350.00

Plate 80
Dog.............................$65.00
Swan, white...............$250.00
    amber $165.00
    clear $125.00
    transparent blue.....$200.00

Plate 81
Chicks on oblong basket,
    white....................$325.00
Chicks on round basket,
    white....................$175.00

Plate 82
Baby Moses $220.00

Plate 83
Rabbit, white $350.00
    clear $210.00
Dear, white $250.00
    clear $155.00
Hen, white.................$250.00
    clear $155.00
Not Pictured
Beaver, white.............$850.00
Lamb, white $450.00
Dog, white.................$300.00
    clear $200.00
Baboon, white.........$1,200.00
Frog, white $500.00
Monkey, white.........$1,200.00
Dining Pig, white......$1,200.00

Plate 84
Rabbit, white $65.00
Chick, white $50.00

Plate 85
Small turkey, white.......$45.00
Ribbed rooster on lacy base,
    white......................$95.00

clear.....................$95.00
purple slag $75.00
other $95.00

Plate 86
Monkey & Hen Top

Plate 87
Bird, white...................$10.00
Turkey, white $130.00
    clear........................$45.00
    clear frosted............$55.00
    other.......................$45.00
Small Hen, white $10.00

Plate 88
Swan Creamer & Sugar
    Bowl, white $45.00
    blue $55.00

Plate 89
Large Standing Turkey,
    clear $250.00
    small.......................$25.00

Plate 90
American Hen, white $70.00
Cannon on Drum,
    white......................$80.00
Not Pictured
Cannon on Kettle Drum,
    white......................$70.00

Plate 91
Remember the Maine,
    clear........................$50.00
    white.....................$110.00
    green $90.00
    blue $85.00
    amber $85.00
    canary...................$100.00

Plate 93
Uncle Sam on battleship,
    white.......................$65.00
    clear........................$50.00

Plate 94
Uncle Sam on battleship,
    blue (repro) $35.00

Plate 95
Dewey on tile base,
    white.......................$50.00
Not Pictured
Dewey on patriotic base,

white......................$120.00

Plate 96
Battleship Oregon,
white.......................$55.00
Battleship Newark,
white.......................$55.00

Plate 97
Battleship Maine,
white.......................$75.00
light purple..............$80.00

Plate 98
Brick Schoolhouse,
white......................$85.00
painted $110.00
Fainting Couch, white ...$80.00
painted $90.00
Log Cabin, white..........$65.00
painted $110.00

Plate 100
Royal Coach, white.......$85.00
Football, white..............$65.00
Baseball, white.............$25.00
Golf Ball.....................$25.00

Plate 101
Fish, white..................$185.00

Plate 102
Sad Iron Butter Dish,
colored transparent ..$55.00
Cookstove Butter Dish,
colored transparent ..$55.00

Plate 103
Donkey Powder Jars,
clear.........................$15.00
pink $20.00
Elephant Powder Jars,
clear.........................$15.00
pink $20.00
Lovebirds Powder Jar (new),
clear..........................$7.00
colored $7.00

Plate 104
Swan Powder Jar $15.00

Plate 105
Powder Jars,
Bambi carnival $20.00
pink $20.00
poodle carnival $20.00
Scottie carnival $20.00

Plate 106
Lady Powder Jar, clear
painted $25.00
Milady carnival Powder
Jar, marigold $35.00
Two Elephants Powder
Jar, clear $25.00

Plate 107
Duck Soap Dish, clear ..$15.00
carnival....................$20.00

Plate 108
Old Abe Jar, white $125.00
Owl Fruit Jar, white....$140.00

Plate 109
Bull's Head Mustard Jar,
white.......................$175.00
w/ladle...................$250.00

Plate 110
Bull's Head Mustard Jar, repro,
purple slag
(no ladle) $35.00

Plate 111-118
Reproductions for comparison

Index

Schroeder's
ANTIQUES Price Guide

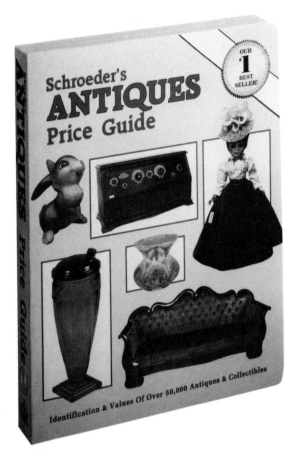

Schroeder's Antiques Price Guide is the #1 best-selling antiques & collectibles value guide on the market today, and here's why . . . More than 300 authors, well-known dealers, and top-notch collectors work together with our editors to bring you accurate information regarding pricing and identification. More than 45,000 items in almost 500 categories are listed along with hundreds of sharp original photos that illustrate not only the rare and unusual, but the common, popular collectibles as well. Each large close-up shot shows important details clearly. Every subject is represented with histories and background information, a feature not found in any of our competitors' publications. Our editors keep abreast of newly-developing trends, often adding several new categories a year as the need arises. If it merits the interest of today's collector, you'll find it in *Schroeder's*. And you can feel confident that the information we publish is up to date and accurate. Our advisors thoroughly check each category to spot inconsistencies, listings that may not be entirely reflective of market dealings, and lines too vague to be of merit. Only the best of the lot remains for publication. Without doubt, you'll find *Schroeder's Antiques Price Guide* the only one to buy for reliable information and values.

8½ x 11", 608 Pages   **$12.95**

COLLECTOR BOOKS
A Division of Schroeder Publishing Co., Inc.